continuations 2

Douglas Barbour and Sheila E. Murphy

continuations 2

 THE UNIVERSITY
of ALBERTA PRESS

Published by

The University of Alberta Press
Ring House 2
Edmonton, Alberta, Canada T6G 2E1
www.uap.ualberta.ca

Copyright © 2012 Douglas Barbour and Sheila E. Murphy

Library and Archives Canada Cataloguing in Publication

Barbour, Douglas, 1940-
　　Continuations 2 / Douglas Barbour and Sheila E. Murphy.

(Robert Kroetsch series of Canadian creative works) Poems.
ISBN 978-0-88864-596-8

　　I. Murphy, Sheila E., 1951- II. Title. III. Title: Continuations two.
IV. Series: Robert Kroetsch series of Canadian creative works

PS8553.A76C653 2012　　　　C811'.54　　　　C2012-900189-9

First edition, first printing, 2012.
Printed and bound in Canada by Houghton Boston Printers,
Saskatoon, Saskatchewan.
Copyediting and Proofreading by Peter Midgley.

A volume in the Robert Kroetsch series.

The University of Alberta Press is committed to protecting our
natural environment. As part of our efforts, this book is printed
on Enviro Paper: it contains 100% post-consumer recycled fibres
and is acid- and chlorine-free.

The University of Alberta Press gratefully acknowledges
the support received for its publishing program from The
Canada Council for the Arts. The University of Alberta Press
also gratefully acknowledges the financial support of the
Government of Canada through the Canada Book Fund (CBF)
and the Government of Alberta through the Alberta Multimedia
Development Fund (AMDF) for its publishing activities.

Canada　　　　**Government
of Alberta** ■

 Canada Council　Conseil des Arts
for the Arts　du Canada

For Sharon Barbour
DB

To Beverly Carver
SEM

xxvi

burnt haze   lost
thought off   hills
catchments of brittle
lightfalls fall into groves
grown into autumn
s cooling once bronzed skin

those earthen colours offer
muted fragrance
softer light when
hills mirror sleep,
thought fallen though grown
quiet with the finished leaves

leafed through   dreams
solidify / earth transformed
pottery so translucent
mirrored light lays
the late green through
its walls as if a book opening

to text
dreams / pottery / earth
still free to vary
mirrors green shoots
springing from early day
transformed to known lucidity

but know how / or where
of this or that   told
through the ever longer nights
of free walking under woods
words fading into mist or
falling snow untraced there

straight line across these forms
of words / their fading
to a whisper known only
when walking / a diminuendo
mirroring the falling
mist of instances

crossings of no words
land reflecting a green
gaseous gaze contemptuous
where language no longer
lingers even in slight
light of the fallen (s)now

now slight longing tempts
screening of seamed worlds
fallen in language gazed upon
reflection crossed with light
that lingers where land
evens found tempo

thrum tones wound / but flower
traced from under
tempo past the power
of ten a wielding lance
thus parsed beyond
a drum / the drum / of numbing

disconnection   no beat
of heart against fear.
to think to feel
the smallest red glow of
petals unfolding such un
written stories thrumming the air

fear assigns a hearse to
even the most glowing petals
stories of heart unfolding
so justice is undrummed
to points of disconnection
thought written in midair

on the breath of a whisper
ed scream for help   carried
by another stretcher bearer
filling the trucks hearsed
to grave resistance / how
think toward the unknown dead

fills page after page, leaf
after leaf falling steadily
rained upon / words dark
ly spot them / smoke
the crimsoned air for

seen grounded

swept clean via
there there therapeutic
ally to blasting s bloody
blessing of the new seed
ed ground / all flesh
grained / lifting to clear sky

clear lie clear spy traced
seed drafted to
unbless the blood
the ground the rapier
twisting past taste into
a once settled earth

settling unsettled as all
ways colonial virus
captures open room after
mansioned glade burning
clear land to seed
with blood grown rich

yearning bloods the ram
page toward span of
cauterized dismantling
of and via
seeming scansion
previously rich and open

turns & turns as re
verse moves around
those blasted heaths
heather burnt clean
they say that
they say that death is clean

lean earth stays
that lay of land
earned either lasting
found terse
slinging burns
louvred without sound

into such a prison
housed language of
earnings levered through
burnt wi(n)dows burning
bushes slanting down to
river s edgy wandering

cut sharp in huge stone
roads / signs / signal
cut & thrust of
armies taking each road
bloody burned / language
retreating word by word

letter in blood /
cut stone / sharply
defined armies thrust into
thought that burns
to form huge roadsigns
stripped from living / language

seen by marching or
stumbling 'folk'
a pilgrimage of fire
where no birds sing
nor human voices more
than moan in giving shape to pain

5

gesture matches shape
of human giving
in the march mode pilgrims stammer
while awaiting a command
wholly without song
with birds not near

xxvii

chorus after chorus
scales a staff of wires
birds reinvent each moment
an apparent gift
breath wings into
knife blue sky

backhand a way
into the wires of reinvention
moment brushing moment
across time becomes a chorus
one hums apart
from breath blue

steal away 'my' heart
into blues wing & sing
back up scaling heights
breath breaks against
wave upon wave to reinvent
brushstrokes sky untuned

& dive from diva wing
(s)ing it into ocean s
drum on rock / rush
of intake in & ex
halation slow & gathering
momentum into world

beaches and hooves / again the roof
of science breeches cross
swooned melodies
rhythm lifted to the heard
an instinct green to blest
sweet tilling of the rest

third trellises beneath the rain s
wheat fill looming
transience with remembered
place on roof tops
tines of rain against
green blessings

heard melodies & rhythms
are sweeter still / swoon
of trans science touches
on lift   drumcall across
forest roof / the green
blest / or bled (blasted

grown   windblown against tin
roof s rattle & drum
jazzed melody
combers break
against the scarp
to scale the green interior

7

rhythming in wave
lengths of green wash &
sparkle thrummed
down / oil slicked
sludge sound fudges
waterlife dead into crevices

beside another life
a muted spark sounds
faint green rhyme
with spores wave down
the lengths from
crevices as mere form

hanging gardens of
sparring spores shelfed
on washed rocks
standing against spillage
spoilage / green opposition
to deep and surfacing black

grablight finding wood one
tendril at a time through
push from under
placates tow and slight
cracking of place
and tended light

a little crawlspace
owns the glow encircling
wide cave
atmosphere moist as
limber bough
finding a place

watching the shadows prance
against far wall
ed presence presenting
as disease / as if in
tents desire played out
lined against the night

in tents the shadows
pace night shorelines
far against desire
lining the night wall
far into presence
toward its ease

easily the night outside
or too bright day
blinds as well
pull them down / let
no fixed idea escape
predicted presence

let blinds cease to
predict the night / the fixed
daylight guide easily /
escape the pretense
of ideas / allow the pull
of pulse to draw in close

the move to bodied
thinking that the rider
on that contract means
no more than clear
eyes can see ears hear
skin take pulse of skin against

clear skin hearing eyes
bodied thinking
ridden move to tracts
of flight in pulse
means thought no more
than with still taken

in / tracked on skin
the pulse lips sense
winging across such scapes close up blue
rivers map & pump
across tan undulations

motion maps such winging
as percepts a way not perfectly
capable / the pumping of
pulse crosses and tracks
a day / the day
close up offers a scope

tele / or micro
scopic topography
gently trembles to
every thrum
of loving drum
driving the bright blood on

the drive against and with
drum s kin stretched
blood and thrum
beneath a scorching sun s
bright scope that chastens
every trembling

leaf through pages
living maps of life
throb & pulse of
DNA images images
a desert scape blown
beneath the chastening sun

swirling rumours played replayed
and pulsed with maps
of chaste moments prior
to the leaves and scars left
by their falling
captured in a scape then magnified

scattered scars magnify
the rolling landscape
s slash and burn
slowly gone down
the few leaves left
fall on barren ground

ground figure relationship
the curve where burn was
and a landscape holding
still follows now dried
leaves drawn into earth
quiet and scarred

xxviii

slight twine s kin scat sing s
littering the forest floor
pale gray with leaves
and ice and overhead
the clouds cross quiet
with their spot song rolling

notes fall like snow
through the thin air
scattered not littered
there of what s clouded
ice rings transparent
leaves held in firm in form

unheld in air and fading
clouds in lost ph(r)ases
moving into transparency
each word 'leaves'
scatters toward mulch
memory crunch frozen

shadows of trees recall
each leaf archived
against the trunks believed
as such / as signs
in silence tell
tales of past present

present signs redeem small
centres until quiet
leaves the shadows plain
where they were placed
as broken ones now older
admit the early days

so far lost early works
and days gone into white
fog or snow / a fall
ing off   shadow
less sun signs vague
darkness of leafless woods

scent of smoke wherever
scent of snow
an early walk across
white fall shadow
wood and days
in fog vague darkness

a sound like shush to vie
with seasons clash   iced
in sheets of white lace
brittle as meshed
in breath that steers
the sand meridians

beneath each breathing
long line walked in melody
the susurrate sand
shakes rhythm steering
into mists turned to fall
ing snow squeaky clean

soft swollen sand shaken
from wind lifts lines
in breaths of mist a melody
elapses surfaces
while walking shifts
the seas and seasons

slipped and felled / arm
up to the elbow grasping
mere grains of starshine
turned and   raising
a new self out of history
s grasp unfolding once again

a new self upholds
shine of stars
these grains unfolding
slippage fades
again each grain remaining
salts away a place

as new selves flake off
turning into hidden
caves / salted or
shining   still slippery
falls felt in the bones
fading into various tunnels

skin peels and the under
layers slip to bones in various
hidden spates of salt
and shining felt
to fade as new selves
chafe against old atmosphere

burnt & burning still above
the now glassed desert sands
who hidden in caves below
shredded flesh hanging
reaches each new self up
beyond the thousand suns

staves encompass charred
sounds that included pines
when young a form of flesh
beyond stunned silence
of glass once sand before
the reach would yield a desert

as if a clearcut through pines
the blast brightens then
chars the now stone ground
forms framed in light
then dark / an afterimage
flash against stone stunned

as each tree falls
in silence framed
crime unheard   un
recollected   blasted
pine replaced a larger
green growing thing gone down

and green replaced
the thought of green
the thought of green
grew silent as a crime
replaced each tree
unheard as fallen

dream falls forward
into daylight stripped of thought
less ashed autopsy
to a drunk dance
among trunks
no longer there

top shell trances
fallen thought no longer
green dreamed forward into
ashen seams of stiff
dance slim to tall
drunk s passing sleighs

s lids he said whole
heartedly while slipping
through drifts of words
blown through trees for
forest burnt and layered
in ash / or is now

a tension to or at
burnt edges slip
pery slope shifting
underfoot / brush
away a moment
s hesitation borderlined

between again are edges
sloped to /
moments after
hesitation lines
a place to place
the foot begin / the shift

xxix

moment aery slopes of
windshift hesitation / winged
wobble / whoosh of
slipstream slide in
the between a gain
each foot placed takes up

spaced / expanse / the slide
from leeway into recognition
watch the ease / gain
part of the invention / and between
each placement / taken up
the slopes with care / with silver

invention s torqued flight
light soaring tension s
dance lends slope
to lance / the slaking of a core
blanched from tall mussed breadth
of these laved springs

17

or bubbling or falling
water laves each
core sample dug deep
into the wound
circle of torn trees
moss rock / slackened now

seams of rough greenbrown
slashed down to stone
seeping / steeping
temporal quick
bloodwork
darker ever in the blue air

tones brown the stash of winter s
dark veil lowering
to prior blue
air seaming the rough
hewn forest and the moisture
steeping simply down

deepwater holding back
wafts of steam / snow
blow up / the downfall
summer s gone green
seaming lack as forest
s smokey murk reveils

rift fades / white whelmed
held over / traces green
up from the roots / to slope
and out often / where slide
moves filled / with lift
toward silver chance

slipsliding silver traces
blue now into earthgreen
[d]rifts / fragments
gone down / gone down
rooted blossoms stumbled
upon dreams fade / falter

rifts turn to dreams
grown blossoms falter upon
blue divides each
fragment roots the slips
of fathoming green
peeled to sky and light

touched face rock powering
aside after aside the resonance
of storm that dusts over
rage seeking years .
gone / years coming forward
to offer green / to light

to climb as fingers
etch possible routes up
clutched as whipped dust
storms stone citadels .
clung to in darkness fallen
on green shoots lost in cracks

can growth articulate
a vision quietly gone down
to sandblast lightblast
dune or rock faced
green outline of some
probable thing or being lost

and in the pause / a form
of relaxation calls upon
that nothing / subsumed
under a pieced light
smattering around
white valleys

seeming rush or wash of
always new step or turn
of wheel worked with
heavy hand / un
walking / snagged in snow
striving into the moment s slash

lashes catch the half
moist wash of turning
while the walk is
heavy on each step
the hand steers part
way noticed in the blend

whiteslap catches the eye
en passant   hemisphere wrapped
in cloud desertstormed
as windcharge
sideswipes small motored
wheels for wounded egos gone

loud swipes mall
heels slapped by
spheres hushed toward
a tall eye gone
to clouds as
wrappings en passant

long caves blast light
tamp land s blurred
calm / height
at which stone shows
the craft of centuries
as tall lapses

of philosophy / that love
fallen into the sun
down the lit slope blurred
lapsed craft constructs
stoned honour / as
slope s calculus paints

thought of stoned crosses
sunned in space aflame
with rapt calls
taking their cue from
honour s glories
blurred as spun

honour off the fire
flares ever higher
flashpoint of escape
from gravitas dead weight
rhetoric gone silent
in the fast expanding void

that shifts as though
material inflected with
points of rhetoric or scope
sequential flaring across
floors as gravitas
desponds its way to form

as flow of body shift
inflects each gesture
downward / material speech
arguing floor and wall
fall into the far beyond
all possible touch or sight

sway   fro

sense supposition

s reach / stretch

to stay upright

inflects each gesture

into grace as fall

summarily a place divides

into the senses

as upright inflection graces

fall and reaches tips

of the branch grown

orderly not wild

xxx

knot glowing moonlit
ripples into dark woods
scatter fault lines
places beyond green
written in wind
mind s fall with hush

track every fault
line up with righteous
anger or blues nota
bene: crewel pain
darkly inked impressed
stone shadows climb

limbs shallow listless tones
pressed sinking stark
where train tools rain
rote jewels tangled
in tight pine
vaults very lacking

red & brightening
lights / rote nation
turned and caught in
vaulted aporia
apparitions trace trance
into enveloping cloud

look how these
apparitions seem to
show some other
trace about them
caught and rote and
vaulted still enveloping

such high silence
ghost traces swirl in grace
less sound less sight
in daylight against snow
light falling etched against
vaults of shadow deepening

races to swirl a round snow
flutters the deep centred
light with globe of glass
around as vault with hope
toward high within
a ghost of sound pitched fallen

as seen from far above
snow stranded and
held static in air gone solid
in light / frozen
ghost flash of unthought
burdening the berserker mind

slant how truth
full fills what taken
stance   static   fallen
to icy distance   calls
cold and hard (heard)
buried on the line

all to iced distortion
call callow herds of
buried lines leaned on
aslant how dances in
the attic fold to
aching full and lard

loud active louting
echoes rime like
beneath the sea / stone
intel slanted into
belief gone dead
between those dark doors

tele pathetic lone lead
darkens sea vanes left
in stone to echo paler
taintings between
death and locked
inactive recollections

phased and phrased out
words shadow stone concrete
memories taint traced
too faintly grained
as dark waves shear cliffs
toward new achieved loss

the act of carving paces
beyond traces and encumbers
dark words phrased
to concrete as achieved
acts leave behind all
recollection parsing loss

as carved beauty shaves
off sandstormed / blasted
beyond bitter before fear
grounded in mist
ghosted in guesswork s
grammar of grieving gone down

fear at the precipice
of erasure via sand
recalls the ghost
of grief and carves
a beauty misted over
fraught semblance and storm

in fright a bitter light
stumble into the
looked down upon / locked
into tunnel vision
the ghosted dark echoes
dauntless horns screaming

looking up into the bitter
tunnel horns clash
a metallic teething
fright skitters formed fear
sparks echo screams
infinitely repeating

metrognomic groundfire
echoes through tunnel
after tunnel vision lost
in smoke and mirrorflash SOS
repeating engine roaring ever
more massive at the fearful eye

one mirrors fear the sound
repeating massive roaring
past the eye that echoes
groundfire more
smoke fails to mute
loud fear as engine after engine

grows in eyepiece ever closer
ranged in rows running
wild across abysmic dark
sands stretching etern
in terms dataed black
warding carpetbagged bombs away

running the ward with car
pet dark in strands pieced
ever ranging grown abyss
to stretched term (in)
all ingredients bagged
shut and with/in range

bugged & baggy trousers
dance down darkened
halls   blooded animals
trail the siren s sound
feet slipslap on abysm s
edgy reach / (st)retch of

the real down deeper than
infinite symptoms branching
back to a fundamental
thoughtless blood
eternally invaded
as changed

xxxi

altered eyes sea altered
states stratified while futures
dig their way through layered
romances weight of
battle bought off
in widescreen sandstorm

the view weighs less than
what is there the battle
is too visible as strata
lining romance of the wide screen
storm that will not
sting the eyes

whose crinks against
the smallest stone
thrown up / burning
come as passion romances
each dig into layered histories
pages turning to what sight

hidden or obvious results
spawn like replay of history
to locate stepwise pre
sent moment in sequential
logic unaccustomed to
an unplanned flowering

untaught buds balance
on a day s sad honesty
sun might shine news
might come ungurued
in the garden gone
to sand and explosives

dust smarts ingrown roughage
sand downs the path to
failure then and if
imagination s only solid
as antipathy and soundly
mimicking browned gardens

a kind of etch the
scratch of miniscule man
ipulation / stipulation
silence   or the shock shook
inner ear sanded down to
flash flesh all smoothed over

afterwards / what
theatre theology theodyssey
reign as adaptation
takes the soul and flesh
into its hunger and
adopts around amnesia

such thought gone down to
unhabitation / capitulation
s new forgetting getting
lost in windblown sands
propellered into blind eyes
trapped beneath the ocratic gaze

faith fully grounded woodknot
forest for trees long de
foliated burns redly against
evening sky darkening as
ancestors soldier away
rivers now sunk beneath sand

on which right there there
seems to be a red spread
ing stain conspiring to carry
sight into trees defoliate
and caught in scopic tendresse
loss fades in the posted trauma

as continuo grows swollen
leaving little place for
recollection and the trees
reddened by day s scope
equal to the moment
fading apart from sight

and sound reaching after
rage   counterpoint / under
the (l)eaves / bored
walked to dance of
bones   branches Asche
Asche all fall down

walk / the dance / all fall
bored into under
bones rage to a whispered
counterpoint in thin
sound after branch
on branch turns ash

prescribed rest in nestled
compass of branched vessels
scared or scarred lung
flight / seared breath
burns the darkening air
ash or mist filled falling

nest nestled compass
darkening as mist
to fill scarred script
burned in fall approaching
each branch to soften
fill of light

the screen sifts script
into falling ash   dark
lines of flight flat
against fiery sky
black timber teeters
toward some new notation

pronounced fire thoroughly
unsifted lines gain on
screen sight a matte finish
sky slimming dimension
timber partly black
tests simmered light

duration or durability
incised remembering
adds weight and stress
to moving flambeaus
shadow engraved buried
thought forgot and re enacted

act supplants movement
s prior stark line
chiselled on thought
that lasts though buried
recall weighs something precise
ly equal to nothing

the knot (nought) untied
slips material bonds weight
less than spectre letter
lighter than conjecture
winging above clouded
maps of a market yet to arrive

plain as rust felt
spectre in the hand
lighter than thin
wheel tracing on map
the places knotted
in bonds so gradually unwoven

xxxii

missed   misted desire
reaches out through branched
ways shaded and chiaroscuro
mapped territory laid
far beyond its own limits
as spectred time tends to grow

lone fence lines specks
of imitation toned past
aged apt charred vase
on ranch time too tilled
ire lifted to mist
and territorial in time

listing as if waves froze
across the horizoned white
land rising or falling slow
lie of cut saplings criss
crossed to denote temper
airy possession / its speed of loss

as saplings slow to white
horizon dims to frozen
speed of loss chalking
air across waves crossed
as if fences tempered
the tone of falling

33

through eons / or light
years behind any slow
sun s glow   erring mediated
atmosphere freezes
the booted stance compelling
bright bits of information down

thrown trance eases low
light s bright years
through atmospheres shifting
the compilation of info
infra tactile slow boots
merchanting along their trace

transfers or transforms
chance elements of neoned
night to day rounds reactivated
as light shakes the cloudy
air below an eye meaning
only to purchase a hold   a whole

as if a cluster / animations
acting out their emulations
of offered and
yet how such (un)realized
glowing projections move a
beyond desire trapped therein

lustre fields inanimate the act
of glowing moves beyond
traps offered and then realized
with gain projected on
identified desire for
pause between the greens

passing fair / or far
leaves foray trapped light
lit out for such territory
where extreme away casts
a line of twink all
flicker toward the grave core

spelled wrong   or misunder
stood beneath so much green
reach / through doorways
juddering between worlds
driving across possible
high ways caught between flickers

a quiver wrought in tension
squeezes out of focus
one shrill truth achieved
from in between the pass
age of apparent door
ways leaning well and green

leading wall and groan
of opening way / a rusty
lack of trusting possibility
shutterspeed dilation
lenslight reaching to
lay the stargleam on it

how to hold a pose
position possibility as
truths spread slowly through
an evolution of light itself
etched quietly onto wide plates
stretching perhaps the scene

through pose   self
shrinks a posse distance
etchings quiet across
slow scenic plates
evolving into
a positioned truth

or many / their wild
chase through space
or time / what s lost in
canyons   shadowed
abyss of non remembered
sureties   the force of

simple plants transcending
space around them
faithful to core shadows
buoyed by depths
that texture the abyss
time wraps around these multiples

each flowering moment opens
into brighter minim
all given to rising colour
up from / out of
dark deep hold back
as if those thoughts could not fly

rising tones imply
their depths amid ephemeral
impressions plural and between
lines partially assigned before
relaxing into thought
that lasts as inclination

to dance out
from gravity s sombre hold
toward some never
reflected signs of lit
tel quel illumination
fractured in each small splash

clarity invites belief in
permanence after tiny evidence
reflects desire made whole
in movements that pass
with a simplicity equal to
fractures added up to gravity

lipped upon the farther shore
tipped in slosh & fall
ing pebbled roar / the reach of
moon pulled grave desire
turns reflection s legend
that fragmented line of light

pieces fall into reflections
of the legend being made
from motion and the space
between gestures in which light
tips reach and lines
form between desire and shore

xxxiii

a silver reach across the line
shored up or sheered away
to depths darkening
as if space itself reached out
in some trans for mat
aerial flip those wings forget

matte finish mutes the sheen
of surface transacted
to its depths
reached for then shored
beneath a tip of cloud
lining that clarity

carried across the silver edges of
or furred as if
to give protection
which wind brings change
shaping tatters anew so fast
or shoreline s ledges over aeons

fast or s low the ledges
shift as wind is more
reality than furred surface
that silver shaping of a line
another change
once crisp then tattered

running   or rolled across
the pebbled sight
lines shored along the shift
ruffled indeterminate sur
cease scrying edges blown
awry   flecks of silver strewn

edges trace history no
longer in sight the shore
determines what is washed
beyond retrieval silver
rolled and pebbles
smoothed by warm then chill

archived heat and cold trace
histories lost in wash of
sounded clash returned
through repetitions roll and fade
of pebbled palimpsests play
out indeterminate lay of land

the fade of play means
movement come to stillness
thus sound must be repeated
to be lived
the pebbles quiet
and the chance archived

carefully read
stacked   stocked
rockrepeats re: pealed
and belled strange
attracters lines of
flight   flickering doors open

range of momentum comes to
speech without the words
still recognizable as full
syll tracking re/cognition
one dot at a time
to form an open line

all vowels and consonants
fragmented by the pain
hope less than fear s
a predicate predisposed to
loss / lack s witless
crush on what s believed to come

each thing afforded its small
ration threaded through
the whole confined position
inked into the psyche
facets of which impact
upon the darkening facts

as if impressed and
then slow motion pulled
through emulsion to sight
ration all faetual but for such spin
as machined distraction can impart
answers to questions no one asked

thirst s excess dreams away
the factual spun rations
as if pulling from objects
neither objectivity nor objection
and apart from a conceived
machinery impressed upon the quest

ions pulse through machined
momentary charges neither
objective nor object of
a torqued inquiry into
origins / organization
all gone from world s light

or moment seaming the divide
between inquiry and torque
shifting organism from
turn to pulsed machine
this | this | this | this
metronome endeavour starting

each moment startling there
then | then | then | then
never returning knot
ched pain cracked
tribulations engine
churning manic on that heath

engines transpass their
turning manic across
acreage with/without re
turning manic over h
ills the pain of moment s
being constant and eternal

internal wash of rush of
crush of crack
t crippled creak of
all a float can bear
upon such hills as green
groan peaked and shatter / fall

prey to | praying rip
pling over green
crush of soft hills
interiors brushed
fine to floating
waves this lush

as if washed silk
surrounds the body
breaking out to breathe
anew the salty air
white tanged tinged
with chill and cutting edge

hushed fabric of atmosphere
forms white erasure
sharp to tips of wings
porous / untainted
by surrender
to the field of thought

and feathering fealty
fliffs almost silent
lift into whiteout raised
etching against fading blue
reach of for unto some more
than single fragged mentation rising

whiteout chipped a
way so what visiblates
is form
er blue frag still
not full though single
mental quiet raised toward r/eaching

xxxiv

in sudden silence sight
refuses to know
wings feather fragments
of fog aside into
a woof and weft whitely
blending tears against wordhoard

impartially situated in
an ethered brightness
blended strands / the DNA
of discourse coursing
through high canyons
riven misty indices

crayon works indent
the discourse after
ID ing sectors of the blend
as if science
were comprised entirely
of impartial louverings

archived Louvrings / leavings
layered colours over
hidden hectorings / vectors
informational parquet
lengths of scraped clean
hide a seeking eye deciphers

across the length of vectors
hidden information [scrapings]
layered ciphers form
as though first seen
first thought
sans colour [leavings]

scrapings toward
some bright future lack
ing history s accumulations
archives of time passed
each faded colour a little
later thought thunked down

beyond the gerund of snap
shot, slim colours
a little faded form
a frame thought plenty
bright to show
the archives passed

will it last in colour
or will it be black and white
how held or framed
will plenty place itself
against the grain of
rivering time cutting deeper

deep(ly in) grained place
sense gains timed river
holding the last colour
squeezed from blackandwhite
versus prior blankness
itself a form of will in frame

over time as passing
images sail that current
too fast / fade against
the grain of shadow
and light taken solid
and delicately laid on

on raised or delicate platform
shaken pain the speed of current
means no image sails
the passage leaves a shadow
ingrained in
an exact light

bread on the waters
shakes in freckled light
sinks beneath rippling
musculature hidden
rivers shadowing head aches
angsts exacting precision attack

muscles shadow the expanse
of water / hold recollections
rippling beneath immediate
recall as rivers grow
continuo to aching
as precise as any natural line

of flight or light versed
in the contrast contralto
stream of notes flowing
carrying each ache bent
nota bene memorized
map mundane overflown

crisscrossing palimpsestic
riverruns canyons built
citations rung (wrung)
from rock and sand
swiped wheels turned
and held there centuries

wrung cities turn
to held ones   rock
crayoned onto canvas
crosses centuries
and sand runs
where the water

stops as cut into as
ridiculous formats in stone
stun the eye / left there
archived   or broken
ozymandiased cults
draped across cavern walls

toned crayon covens still
the eye awhile left   .
clear as cut stone
held postponed across
walls and screens
and claiming acts of archives

whither wither colours
caressed across rock
walls hidden deep who
cut and fleshed icons
lifting toward spirit
s covened desires

icons not flesh covered
desires deepen walls
cut shrill from lifted
rock across a
capsized wish
in colour s coven

clarity s layover
between flights
and images require
liftoff to reveal
their prior shapes each
letter risking being crushed

across the seals
word fathoms yield
mere riff looming
part cache
part beyond
presumed syllabic ceiling

to break through   gl
as so or up ward off
weird oaf s no part of
muse sick harmony
riff raft trailing
bubbles broken behind

47

thick breakage trails
of glomming on   are goals
implanted   does harmonious
fluencia low its way to part
ascension part
beneathment spoken

broken routes dug
into stone ascents
lead on to hoped
for stargaze / redly
shining so close
the one planet calls

opacity absorbs the nudge
of light / the act of shining
is propelled by hope
as if a planet served
as answer to the question
why ascend

xxxv

is it miracle time yet
are we cuffed to a robust
form of the water coming
down below its prior level
shaded by tradition
and its white stones

or can a miracle last
that long   to cut
its way through stone
glowing in morning
and evening light
transgressing eons

time might shuttle its own
weight beyond the lift
of small lights flecked
against stone cut from ages
evening the flow
of miracle as seen / not seen

such sly dis
appearances / sonances
sung softly into curves
of rock cracked light
catches   notes bent
through speed of descent

caught on a slice
of colour sharp
ly sheered to whiff
waft of / dance of
light thrummed basslines
thumping up and out

a bluer thin sense
savored pale against
the constant thrum
in softer tense
drumming the precipice
of chance lift off

or sheer crash & wash of
quick shove of hull
or airframe / all move
mentate a medium
thick with soundings
wrack and crack s song

spot motion thickens wash
in point of fracas where
the medium small evidence
goes surely placed
with hull and habitat
as friction leaving trace

saving place fought through
to / as drip and scrape
push colour into flattened
possibility / caught
in the moment
airy mediun as if sailing

flat posse searching
point by point caught
in the pictured save
a moment s air left placed
versus the sail
the sailing

how the moment
s held in thrall
temporal notation
wind in sails balloons
foam flecks white
against distant darkening blue

white is sails in
motion flecks of
distant moments held
against temporal notes
suspended foam the darkening
balloon still rising

raising red possibilities
notes flow as cornucopia
utopia of sound boom
balloon filled hot
and into light or dark
er blue bent to blow

darkening low moments
situate the cornucopia
within range of siege
the colour fierce
red grapples with
leftover blue

fading falling light
drops below the rounded
edge of the world
walls under seige of
darkness   waves
reach towards the moon

rounded darkness coils a
round each edge of fading
moon weighing a slip
waves once reached
siege on siege of winter
in its east formation

ragged armour rages
thin white light spattered
against the fortifications
weightless in gazes
held static in glare
a dark moment gone

when is motion a mere
flash of heat in wind
weighing a concentrated
or concentric rage
and when is glare
in rags thin as a flower

spores blasting every
where reflexive
pain without
the syllables to flesh
out an attention
to declare the shreds

as if from within
that fiery whirlwind
concentric / ashes
flung up and out
a mist of white seed
less loss grows nowhere

wind flung mist
seeds out less fire
centrifugal fracas
jeers the glow no
wherewithal can mete out
loss on white feel with and in

xxxvi

loss or less of white
base / colours slaked
slicked thick across
bands crosses blocks
toward black never
achieved see   that mist

recedes to looms
that weave a definition
complicated as precise
lack stirred into imagined
presence of all colour
that equates to black

digging below that surface
to swathes of colour
dwell or earth
ed in palimpsestic
simplicities conjoined
and rising into lack

yet felt indwelling
or apart shapes spawning
momentum of reflexive
form each trace
equivalent to thought
to dance in space

across dun deserts
of inspiration winds
ex or in hale a future
blown apart on flat
planes of shifting
hues   tones inflected

flats revive the centre
inspiration flexing
bales of hindsight intoned
in an explosive shift
of rays winding around
apart from foreign future

exploded views hung high
flatten perspectives
from dark to light to
mauve glow curtaining
still stacks of wheat
in slow flight from history

still shots render eternity
in small squares
tamp down inherent light
of broad and wide
perspectives aka refurbished
history approaching flight

inside the light
the light   the dark
recedes further inward
a negative glow
squared squats
on the surface tensed to go

apprenticed thinking eases
up on tension after
tension   squares of flight
immersed in a surfaces
become a glow
their own receding

builds the blocks
absorbs the dark
light opens out   as
warm wormed flat
tensed in toward
a surface slow embered

brass instruments show
through the dark tensed
to perform a surface
opening / blocks yield
embers focusing some flat
rationale or other

laid out there to walk
around such rumpled heat
seeking missed fells of
colour drained   drooped
coals turning   as gyred
instance burning   out

the ography of heat
shifts colour to itself
to walk   the act of seeking
misses spells of thought
turned instances
out of the corner of around

ever receding geometrics
in and in and in
smaller yet larger means
follow colour fields felled
through doorways entrance
d by misted distances come close

shapes folded into colour
field the mist beside
receding strains of distance
flecks of passage close
to finish lines felled
entrances equivalent to rest

equivocate with rest
lessness / to enter
through such huge
cloudy windows out
lined misty against
receding walls ever darker

not a thing seems simple
enough that lined entry
offers a measure
of the walls their
darkness and clouds
against a wider mist

that complications inhere
in what s missed among
such darklit corridors
dim incandescences hung
at fading distances among
the static stuttering longueurs

among inherent static
a form that s dim beside
the incandescent content
absorbing distances from teak
perspective gathering some
dots to make a line

to rip or cut along
a bias   as if stone or
wood envelopes all
the shapes slid out
into the scattered
air the sshhh of waves

mere attention seems
to mine surprising shapes
that scatter past
the envelope
the act of tide s
continued fluctuation

xxxvii

whipped and whistled
whittled leaves flash by
wind driven into heaps
that mesh and flow
unto trees thinner shade
shackles of light strewn

runes gift thinner drive
to keeping mesh a flow
through shadows as wind
mimics lashing of p/laces
depth strewn through
the listing trees

the listening tries
the inky slap of wind
and last leaf s rite
of ruin read as thin
king s shadowed stain
laid out against that white

ritual shadows ink lines
onto white as
thin leaves crushed
against the thought
of tapping out a song
percussively as touching starch

59

fell   or falling slightly
slow   each flake of white
whittles the air apart
as thoughts fragment
s float into a distance
drawn in negative space

the act of shaping
fragment into whole connotes
collecting at the edges
distance draws from
mixing opposition
with first thought

best thought?   or flaw
ed flight into trees
for forest falling fast
as each separate leaf
or flame flares up
to serrate eyes irised wide

cut for precision to fathom
meld of dark and light
as code relieves the forest
of collective flaws   opening
separation to the status
of a leaf seen apart from flame

each burning page or bush
turned on to telling
clues   the coded message
massed in flames
the reach of smoke blown
ashes all that leaves

first crushed to powder
under coded page
amassed by telling
after sense of hearing
flame on prior leaves
ash passes

and flees   the flight
across borders un
noted below
coded beyond scriving
falling apart and into
thickening layers pressed

inherent order codes
the parts beneath each
layer of crossed light
fallen on the present
surface forming levels
certified as matter

certain maps match
codes cutting edges
lines linking ridges
backlit angles pitched
against a sky falling
toward snow s lost script

ledges hitch to span
of atmosphere with angles
that resemble parts of sky
of snow   trace of a long walk
free form across
what still is falling

failing as the steps
fill in   a falling
light lost beyond
the ridged edge of
the world tumbling
into white   dark untraced

beneath the umber trace
each step recalled
within a body
lost to failing
world in ridges
just surmised

upon that peak look down
look up   balanced
between dark writing
above   cerulean
mirror below
tracing ending becoming

blue darkened plot
of mirrored cloud
upon above points
tracing quiet
balance upon foundations
just becoming

just ice slowly melts
on such cloudriven peaks
flashing light back up
slippery reflections
mark foundational
imbalance sliding down

flecks melt depths
to low slips
ice glithers
as light lashes
at slow speed
prior balance

wave length through
slow glass whitening
below false step
faltered slide of
sight teased onto
log eyes refused

through steps onto refused
wavelengths glass owns
traces of a faltering slide
sight unseen toward
the eyes deemed easy
with false testimony

the world sees knot
warp and weave of light
traced down the mirror
one way / or diagonal
knowledge no thin place
to stand   rockfalling

how the mark
moves on diagonal
trace   down woven dawn
the way that knowledge
trims experience
that stands   grown thin

xxxviii

so stood before the weave
of light and ochred shade
traced across all senses
reaching out to haul
a hailed reflection
bright expansive grasping

flexing fence lines
around Hades woven into
fabric of each dampened
light ground cover
expanded to incorporate
all trails lacing foreground

stretched away from cavern
openings   steam or smoke
a thin veil against stars
lines of deeper darkness
glyphs groping upward
glimmer striated below

tar holds steps together
steaming   liftoff
openings fare better
than the lines
of smoke beneath
felt glimmer

glass / fasttrack
escapism leads into
paths palpably thinned
between ruled lines of
pillars grown or stone
desire s sterile reach

each puerile fire
unlit retracts the tone
of owned rinds tossed
to pulp from
capers tacked on
to a litmus glass

each small struggling glow
rides the eye peering down
from high gearing down
the scopic rush of
ever smaller atomies
alive inside a slide

change scopes out micro
being 'just one look'
and ever each shifts
glowing to live
astride facts breathed
upon the secret small

wearing thin kinetic
granulate imps
articulate pages
slide ways out of
site / fogged in
beneath bright reflection

benign arch across
momentary hold signs
a sustained momentum
of intelligence lights
the turns of wood
as meaning signs each nest

a light ting   such music
drifts in fragments from
each small housed note
making being singing
held there on the move
as if to fly their bowers

from house to making
held lithe one tone unto
the next one being
motion unto light as if
as if such drifts
themselves were song

as leaves open and fall
into manuscript piles
drifting against
against possible trunks
or pillars reaching
to construct a space for song

lingering beside s/paced
days that drift toward lodging
from in/formal markings
each to measure
recollection structured
via reach and fall

and so to sew a line
laid out upon the whited
field folded held and fit
to be plied   in
tent upon a memory
the lodgepole carries on

paint shifts the ply in wood
and lodging s memorized
on command the white
of first things changed
after the lift is folded
open upon intention

the stretch of it in
tension with the draw
and pull of colour
laid upon that under
white   each layer
thick hues laved

layer upon colour drawn
from lift tensed
closed beneath
a colour and a colour
lodged then etched
to sight

laid out in thicker
hues and tones engulfed
within each other
flickering flatly from
glaze upon glaze
eye impinging through

filling out end
pieces not already
there as surface
does not equal
completion each hue
extracting a suggestion

how to   why to
see it says in colour
fully pulls the eye
in to those apparent
plays of light
flattened shadows opening

lulls the why
a slight says colour
to free plays
lateral how open
all the eye says full
though flat apparently

through fiat apparently
that it shine   a glow
ing string theoried
across galaxies red
or blue shifting beyond
the eyes state meant

the or impinges on
what is already
there in galaxies
if shining string
blue opposite
of fever of intent

xxxix

there s an either
in the ether ored
across a sea of stars
strung out there
an as if of
trailing red or blue shift

limbered by use
these crosswise strings
catch flecks of clean
results shifting the glint
of sea to focused
lines across

stretched   the exercise of
slipstream dancing lights
leaps knightwise
across the windflipped
foam   the whirls
galactic liminally limned

random detection becomes
its own arrangement
a measure of borders
this distance from
the real that hastens
movement toward away

where derangement
slips across the line
left empty in the distance
overseen by eyes in skies
gone black with force
fields of cloudy rhetoric

that place of empty
thought now full
of spite exploding
mindmade space forced
up or out or into
that sly returning gaze

fixed perception turns
absorption lingering in place
the kind of light
that litters darkness
before thought retrieves
a prior known equation

dark thinking
moved from a before
so trapped in prior
planning planted as if
concrete was a garden
blown aslant across sigh(t)ing

growths / cuttings
the force that drives
up not across the pavement
breaks through monotony
to sing green thoughts
shading schadenfreude

history turns pavement
over loss that hovers
stitched in story once
driven green recurrence
of diffuse posterity
amply toned

craft refutes the breaking
of these tangibles
enlisted in a colour
one breathes across
prior to lying down amid
a focused hope

as if a smallest flower
broke through that cement
truth fragmented by life
again insisting green
against blue against green
growing things reach out to

skies and skies approach
the breath of earth
conjoining centre after
centred fragments forming
an insistence matching
likeness after life again

above or below   caught
flow flare of sandsky
covering sky s scarce
light flickers   sol
itary itinerary of
flashflood windswept seams

grit against the sun
sheets scar sky
what flowed now scrapes
blurred seams above
a flare of light
caught swept between

mechanical beams support
light flowing down and out
from sky s huge awning
flared and flapping above
all sighting systems
scraped across red medians

under such systemic observation
what inductive possibilities
unfold as metallic dust swerves
into patterns only
the scientific eye can discern
mirrored there in wan light

ideas and formations hold
a scent distinct from
shrill metallic eyelight
fractions cluster into
wholes eventually scientific
from the swerving first induced

such mapping fractals
eyebeams into new commerce
gathered in a carboned city
square the factored trade
of gravity or whorled
magnetic capital gone tsunami

carbon loosens definition
of a fractal
immediately gone
to gravity s magnetic
square whorled into
mapping ex post fact

ohed and ahed beneath
a deep sky or drop
t stitch of timed ex
plosives ploited
on a gradient reef
paper thin and reaching

clothed reach   toned
each   sky dropped grade
thin   coy   deep ploy
tithed seeking rash of
the indelible stitched
time and time as gain

as gone before into
an out of reach
the silver languid
surface stretched
the light of distant
solitary glimmer reflected

reach into stretched
surface   silver flawed
to limn a languid
glimmer across
the space
of solitary light

xl

beige stillness offers
a lament to seasoned children
held mid air whose longing
through the winter passes
acts of soft retention
treading memory

into a less sweet wine
somewhat drunk and lost to
purple fall further into white
drift past forested hill up
rise to a portico inward per
vasive votive candles flashed

motive in the ether
on the hill sweet
purple mist above the forest
pointillist less granular
drift quasi lifted
to the picture further inward

land posits thought posits
space and pacing that convey
a level deep levels below
and further to the core
through hewn untangled
lace by lacing

loosely tied together
a world shifts as eyes
pace the surface held
above the layered flow
of colours digging out
the hewn hued spaces sparsed

local space made whole
by seeing out one
layer at a time
fells trees a surface
at a time layered
in shifts brought home

where eyes have it all
figured / and in
warding fissures of light
layed down upon
a forest s muscled tangles
underbrush collage collects

beside blush candles
the recited collect
absorbs what eyes fix upon
layer by trust
all days figured in
under the rest

where ritual lays
such shivering lamplight
into the shadowed distances
arched aisles of wood
or stone fade slowly
with ever darkening will

lamplights distances (slowly)
the wood willed to the aisles
that darken close to stone
as fading ritual falls
disremembered shivering
apart from certain shadow

gathering slow and short
moves throw the light askew
across the drained stone
altering all in a moment
s trace   what came so far
before mere ashes flown

no element departs but
tone alters the view from
moments across trace once
ashen now invisible
continually gathering
moves long short slow to mean

motive means leap across
sideways corridors
of thought laid out in
light and dark tracks
shivered and flickering
from mass to energy gone down

cold places to walk
resist each step   light
plays harmonic with the side
to side endeavour ranging
from press to touch
inventing often corridors

as steel slams shut slams
open unguarded un
connected shadow splay
spawn indecision pass
words in or out losing
sight and sound stretched beyond

when quiet lifts
the single note absorbs
the space that silence
occupied   the passing
intuition stretches
past a loss connecting still

to hold that fading blue
note falling through
corridors tunnelled
into rock and darkness
striped with flickering
torchlight corner after corner

fall into   from each lick
approaching ear the eye
as if the threshold of
dark moment might
resist some of assumed
light s corridor inflection

couriered infection slides
too easily through fire
walls can t stand against
the fierce high note plucked
from the darkest bent blue
twist of wire / grist of ire

piercing tone escapes
precedence only to arrive
unrecognized though known
apart from seepage of intention
as a fierce vibrato chiselling
presumed dark walls

and blush of form
er light recalled has been
erased the dry cloth blurs
all fallen moments
holding tone and tone
as though a melody in splinters

the scene split into
paired perimeters
backdropped toward the
scarred flies lifting
warped horizons beyond
the wings of song afloat

forks in the road a
tilt in voice or song
line run across a void
no longer measured
fenced instead the lilt
of vision twisted beyond hope

line lifted from the page
line tracing the negative of void
forming a fence along
a way of seeing past
horizon and a voice
no longer shaping hope

one seeks to ferret out
a vision or a goal beneath
a palace in production
rising above pillage
flames at street pace
spun from greed

as any accident of battle
cries heard distantly on
sandy hills beached generals
stand upon where orders loosed
from organization blood
into random racked potential gone

distance from sand forms
safe and quiet fiction
as hills chasten attested
reasons for blood for
accidents in acres s pawning
organ ized not random cries

79

rain down from de
forested rock raised up
beyond now hopes or
qui est la bile wrung
with bullet stain on sand
shored now against ruins splash

hope wealths across even
rain down scars wrung
out from shore lashing
the made up forest next
to rock as ruined
speech that stains

stuttered bloodflow
flayed body screens
the centuries default
modish money machine
makes murder morph
to toll tolled desert storms

by default
the body
screens from depth
the misperfume of
a machine
rote murdering each c enter

into the heavy odours of
blood black caverns
each body breaks on
the new walled order
as if a walking bomb still
thought   as if the human fell

tunnelled possibilities reach in
toward the silvered glow/ lights
shadows shiver / blocked factions
factored on screens and broken
microsecond flickers define
a world abstracted into fencing out

b locked traffic recalls skimming
definitions of the duplex abstract
fact or screened for truth split
low into micro licks feathering
the once huge shoulders
now dis solving prior living glow

depthless striated with cons
fusion   how it spun out
of control   the power of
fashion as revenge perhaps
that rhetoric s demand
to mirror perceived enemies

thereby de
fining reciprocity to mean
formation of a venge
ful city (thin)
sprung from mutual (causal)
loss incinerating even power

thus the site of flames
filling the terraced sky
that city forgets the light
supposed to shine upon the hill
keeps false accounts / fearful
bookkeeping throwing power out

power yields erasure of
the lights on terraced
city dusted with keepsakes
that linger amid warmed over
likelihood failing repeatedly
to materialize as recalled

no torches await those seeking
entrance to the tunnelled
heights / dark emptiness
holds loss of memory
a year even thrown away
that political rag video remixed

hiding s the inevitable safe
keeping memory beneath glass
those torched rags receding
into tunnels mixed with re
collected light the argument
held out to entrances

held back to exits
strategies gone down again
st randed cries out against
his god of war warranty
worn thin / how walk
the line in a dark hollowed out

tact reuses earned wounds
walled in to reason s
bleak integral room
turned black still aging
the retained change
from faith to expectation

s tics   rapid fire reports
echoing down corridors black
ened by bombs directed
from reason s deep redoubts
under mountained maintenance
of strait ways / binaried

consecutively spoked chores
grid themselves in deep
a doppler whine of core
temptation static in the mix
of revelations very plural
aural endgame

very plus versus minus un
thinking responses soon
ravage returned re
treats of rockets red
glaring excuses how taking
out takes on the new born savage (f)law

as garbage in is out
rage flows as rivers red
in truth and law now drowned
out by variant excuses
dilating on a flat line
fault line blooding the sand

beginning now to fade
from the predicted washing
rinsing washing yet perceived
as law while being ignored
because the truth is less
convenient than impromptu edicts

xlii

washdays remind that the white
wafts as steam out beyond
the cleansing / moment
airy breath of bleached
probabilities / to scrub
dark truth from the close weave of fact

all right(ed) now   everything
changed   you can breathe
even facts   après reduction
of probabilities   truth steamed
from confusion   repeatedly
arrives plain recognizable   unstained

and ready to hang / out
or ironed so / the years as
the spirit of iron
ing or y / or steeled against
reductive pasts past all
remembered comprehension lost

implements stand there   their use
observes or lifts beyond
taut recipes for built in taste
with a spectrum there
to loosen otherwise strict
history to open or invent another

in or canned content
to sip or drink in grandiose
gulps   take incoherence
e.g.   passing for or as
the unremembered
a token loss of

symptom and of remedy
but there are ways to pass
from moment to another
recollecting loss as so many
sips thereby inspiring
gulps and fear and sealing

wax as moon reaches apogee
how remembering fills
and falls away into the dark
loss of lit terra pro forma
law locks the firma
meant cryptic water lethed behind

high point where magnetic pulse
repels or draws lit darkness
to opposing prophecy as inquiry
posed to the law laureate instead
of any fluid honest locus
of protracted ethics

watch thought
change   unto others   ever after
sloped drawn   place
its taupe   and mist
in present   recollecting
hope as it was   once fresh

life weighs nothing   wisps
alert the eyes to washed
screens after rain brushes
the surfaces slipping into
characters and passing
becomes itself another noun

say sand / blown across
other gravesites / stones
laved thus lose all indent
ed name / there is no
thing memory hold
ing on in silence(d) thought

friction   wears away
the sign   and memory repeats
the dimming thought across
silence   place
sanding the site and
held   and held

locution as location
where the village struts hold
seamed elastic s fall
back lean to weathered
as recalled away and centred
on the tones the intonation

thunder across beaches
booms / a throw of dice
against the dun scapes
scoped in green sights
saying enemy saying
nothing that is nothing there

a patch of speech and then
replacing speech with weather
colour thought   entire
days equal   snapshot after
snapshot   still staccato
of the enemy   the disappearance

thought / to be in / is it
photograph upon the wall
or a mirror only / 'fairest' pol /
of magistrates their breath too
close / the fog of dog of
beware hic ware hic war

surface thatched with dried vine
blurs the night
ensconced in quiet cold
and silver threads spool filaments
leaving rinds of sight
segmented objects found

round the dust (glass) broken
monuments of plateaus
placate an euphemiasma
fog scurrying across hills
tossed up by lies explosions
all sight lost in clouds of of

breaking moments   here lies
a plateau where platelets
turn to monument
formed shattered
images distinctly singular
within pervasive fog

thrown up as steam perhaps
the continents grind upon
each other / ground
cracked / greed wracked
thrust of flood flame flack
flicker along a tsunami s peak

grinding tone on continents
crack open   to flicker
light   to guide whole
sectors of an afternoon
on continents steamed
open via thrust of reach

soft pink dusking the corners
watching all the gulls go by
undawnted rhetorics ratchet up
a windblown dark cloud rushing
above the shadowed crowd
enveloped in simulation

limn the limber lambent cuff
of mood assembling to a crowd
the watch embellished lingo
sparks from Hades
vellum midnight the same
shadows from human light

the link glows in the handset
flippant gest or is it red
eyed bloodsigned contract
CNNed to waiting eyes
whose deal whose cards
whose tablets fall in sign if it cant

blooded story shifts
with incantation
cards shuffled are then tossed
across the table planned
to seem random thus accurate
fair game these real lives

xliii

random acts of shuffled card
sharp cutting edge in
quest of story s end sorry
end game mend game
came closer to the throw
of dice / ghost falter

leaving pause of inter
woven sorrow edged by active
points of story toward what
actually occurred the felt non
random reprimand for all d raw n
lots of dice and cuttings

fell die turn snakes eyes
cut across the straight road to
sorrowed gates of
green baize bone fed bright
eyes turned away from
random actors quick draw

at first unnoticed the moment
um turns and pairs
of eyes observe
and acquiesce   begin to speak
as if   although uncertain of
the cause dead sure of the direction

down the road   straightline
dustblown clouds of
crowds of fallen / books of
smoke and mirrored gazes
gone into the dark / the mark
anonymous self tossed down

aspiration trawls for cloud
as winter mirrors
road s young dust all
airborne selves tipped
to mimetic attitudes
fallen in line

as if lined up for what
photo sin / thesis of
stunted growth / how far
they all fell   felt nothing
but ordered contempt
keeping order on the line

what line felled
contegrity implanted in the
advent of a simu order
keeping worshipped
amid the stillness h
armed

and the manned re
mains of what might
have been hasbeen
habitude how still
life lets the silence grow   .
around the bruised skin

one dwells with/in with shoulders
where the standing
breaks ranks loosens
bruising and the body s
best protection remains
unbroken skin

unspoken kinship brakes
tanks / a bond surfaces
to take a stand there the
here gone wrong gone
on beyond rhetoric
s far l across bare dunes

hold still
ness / stand plan
ted metering the
beyond taken
bonding here spoken
crosswise into distance

horizons fall beyond there
to here it seems to hear
t   as if the take
were solid coin
not counterfeit con/ex
ceptions a beat at a time

per metronome one | two
and on toward vapour
of iron
ic breath fed into scales
for tolerance coin
ci dent with fall in time

fall into absence its
quietude / how take
the pulse of what might
makes inherent   her
rent veil / stripped
bare before the eventual bachelors

infusion also quiet
inheres | eventual
absence absorbing
Lenten quiet a veiled
impulse prior
to r/elapse

re/ turn   to/ ward
noises off / stages of
the inevitable turn
onto that slope now slippery
wet silence / might
be/ yon meditation / medication

tapped into by turns to
ward off silence
where it grasps the lift s
inevitable as stage f
right surface frictioned by
repeated motions of intent

now lost in as if
each complicated move
meant to be right to be there
but beware of the token
excuse / pardon / who
never entered in tension

here recusal stampedes a
cross wildlife left
complex thus tense
around the force in d
rum and par for
in due course / trust

those green leaves   bloody
animal tracks across lanes
of the world speedily re
sisting / fusing
fraction of the funeral
rights of wayward sons

hope ingrained t
races a line of uni
forms where roses are
in full ceremonial view
presumed to beautify
the truth to hide the blood

xliv

unformed capacity for hope
how sing the hunger
ing above the roses all
owed to a deeper red
run below ceremony
s tress / that flow or flaw

resonance lifts hope
to hush amid these branches
a red swatch
of natural selection
tingles to the eye
forming a place

above the seeking eye
strain of stretch of
colour mutated blood
line / live leaves
flash beyond hope
less choices rooted under

laws that tint the act of sight
a live colour
lash after hope as if
aspiration were less than
acquisition in pursuit
of colour

crafted spirally and upward
to enlist form hearted answer
to the beat that resonates
innately to a likely
updrift in the human
range of depth and form

tuned in turned flat
fifth column spinal
rap of words and sounds
mounting higher   bent
notes   bent necks   eyes
straining toward empyrean

design of mount sounding
quiet as though finished
one note upon the next
strain on a par with
lateral sight tuned
to turning spiral

inward twist of fatal
isms cri de coeur up
rising through songlines
gyres into strains of
held notes / held back
reunion of loves instruments

sustenuto mantra lines
the self as ismic tones in
tune with hearted fate
unific this trained water
first in drops and then
the sure glass face

the sweet sweat of cool
condensation / pummel
each note dropping a ping
pang of nostalg / ecstast
ic breakdown / subject to
the arcane tuning of time

line fracture / broke backstory
'not wanted' / tithing
shards of time still chime
hymns and reconcile
Erasmus (brass mussed)
with a common art

to ally with that blind balance
future gone down in
flaming rigs / instruction un
imaginable to minds
cut off from nature seen only
on bright lit screens / unconscious

afloat and alight all twinkling
height and reach for/ward
off earth or ocean how each
intense flash is a forgetting
connections severed   free
falling info dump to the stars

a loss of balance
ends teetering above
ocean chaos search
lighting to compass grid
grind of lenses lance
of laser slicing night

until search peels sheets
of chaos to the point
of compass lanced ends
balancing the fault into which
each lens reveals
an angle of sufficiency

or the angel of sufficient
suffering spreads wings
blinded by a blight
ed landscape / garbage
blown back into the arms
race lifting light unto the stars

whose velocity stings distance
between blackness equal to
infinity where blond spots
of starlight span wings
of the temple of affordable
young angels filled with sight

wings hardened might not relax
unlit from whispers warped by
modest beat lines in the dark
dread / spoked / broad
vocabulary of existence versus
life replete with the refusals

refuse wings against such
hollow hallways just iced
darkness fills / files negate
nothing held sacred and blind
education a memorized cant
fail allure of righteous mess

sacred red stark memo
lined with pacing after
dark the stinging resonance
the lure of lineation tilled
hollow that allows
various nothing to have spilled

grey space around saplings
in contrast hold small strength
against the louvred barriers
these shadows carry / arcs of uplift
as if to hinge above
a cross tipped just this way

overturned and overruled
black to white with no
space between / those windows
of a soul starved of cloud
skies riffled as leaves whistle
down through forested skeins

a ripple of what is / catches
where elements have
become viable as
interstices lacking names
(always inaccurate
approximations)

99

never to be fulfilled
completion still decoys
the crutched mind s eye
so that arrow flies true
if truth lies in such
deprivation of the real / world

into what abyss where the fires
char the twisted limbs of
prosthetic protest / or on
a desert plain the tall man burns
to scrape the civilized skin
from mind s skeleton in chains

one after the next tall
skeleton tests declared
civilization versus actual
life chained to mind
pressured to release
the act of burning

xlv

thinner capacity and further
thinning / minds handheld
smaller thoughts dis
couraged game low point
click barely remembered
back when darkening

thins   or light thickens into
dullness antecedent to
enlightenment / how
the thin king knits a blindfold
to pin a tale on / battens
every hatch / palls bare

threads when plucked make
not a film of music
while the struts on houses
cannot buck the storms
attracted to these likely
targets all a sure thing

why not negotiate the warp
& woof of thin threaded warning
s way that can never be
chosen as scarfed possibility
how steal away when cold steel obeys
the law of war gone awry

standoff the standard
transists from soft gold
to shrill steel
each warmth subtracted
so the few remaining
seem not chosen

just frozen out / or away
a way of dealing the dead
card off the table / tablets
erased / how the words peace
fully fell like those stars
so yellow in the dawn light

yellow as sand
the frozen chores
that sought repair of scars
recall in sallow light
how worlds of us once
tapped erasure of some prior dawn

the fire of the flare
d horizon   all orisons fall
something like leaves scattered
all soul spread abashed / shot
out through the bloody holes
scattered /   centred fire

haloed not hallowed
hollowed out / holoed
silhouette lacking luck
gone down before that flame
supposed to manifest new
possibility not such faith of loss

lurking posses fess up
to holistic inklings
hitched to niche mantralto
preg nancies approaching
halloween complete with
masques distanced from gavel

how empty robes hold up
a body meant to solo
through twists of melody
turned blue / that grace
full dance of justice untried
costumed cozened consumed

harmony tries patience
when it turns to seasonally adjusted
soloing that hankers after other
notes as if appropriating
thereby fattening the sub
stance / dance in costume

dances consume a melody
burning through the season
s flow / as if reason
s flawed arrangement goes
always awry flying home as lost
boy   refuse to grow up

chastises pearl pure reason
able beings for being
reasoned   as arrangements flown
into headwinds of consumption
taking in the nest and discontent to mean
that home is where the f/laws are

flouting others for whose gain
said to be the upper two per
century or millennium
eagle was it flying high
drug of choice force
fed / cant give it up

high two per other cent
of choice mill fed fees
loutish pure or stanched
by whom egalitarian peut
etre mid flight upper
century some sure given

force fed forced dead
weight waiting for an
end andropropelled
by moneys fears / the lack
a daisy calling planted
crawling dented into dark

is there ever enough
presence pretense absence
as one trawls the empty places
for their opposite forced
image fed death before
life s own antithesis the fear

of of of before before
before became just a not
ation of 'the' past so
fixed there as drugged
mind emptied of of
about long gone into

non depth   some
how paced in rugged
knots   a fevered kind of
emptiness   sus
pended a priori
to mean   permanence

the stultified now non
tense of petrify / retro fry
radiate the whips of scorn
as if the god of war
gone AWOL got
philosophy logic (oh feeling

leads to trance to lift beyond
the rancid overlay of crops
across a field   scorn
neglects   who needs
a god of war   pinched nerves
turn spirit to clay

as if tossed sliced shoots
would reach to heav n
there s pity s pittance
thrown down / a kind
of rank loss   soiled
solace   'our' deliverance

left there 'stoned' a photo
opportunity / impunity
lost last chance saloméd
dance to the new directive
defective field operative
code breaking down every where

place nothing w
here something was
and call the nothing something
functional and better than
what was (the nothing)
just because he says they say

xlvi

in rush blush   iced falls in
to slide through arteries of
rock not stood upon / there
s hope in that / that in hope
shatter a shutter opens still
against the flat light laid upon it

darkness frames at first what
little light inlaid could pierce
in theory arteries or one
thin way that stillness holds
apart the single quiet ice
pre surface fall

through slipslide
grace or grimace silent
lies turned inward
groaning rocks ground
through into under
world wantoned before

some larks clean space
above ground and thin
wisps of soft lines
drizzle from the trees
where grace slips
into being worlded

before and aft error
rides a harder blow
bare trees bending never can
sustain / that note boomed
low and cunning / branches
dripping something not named tears

mind in abundance finds
reflection in such flat and
stagnant waters that that gest
ure float beneficent not torn
as bomb smeltering broken
bodies scatter sub lime / liminal

on worn approach reflective
closure plays open upon
a welter tamed for now
lobbed over the net limning
a field of water scented
like rose in mind and real

that susurrus welter water
enraged tsunamis toward what
rough beast pawing sand walls
wailing demons loose from caves
against the possibility of them
selves as drowned sailors discarded

grief graved upon stone walls
mind mendacious into fall
of lie to lie upon the sand
still shifting where the tide detracts
as if each grain knew it
self to roll alone into the sea

act and all tone rains
to sea line taking a lie
down along granular events
to make into alone time
lacking property as barrier
by which to shift the blame

even a sapphire eyed
lupine lopes across action
ed dunes scoping what only
might occur as imaged in
the cave wall lit and studded
with stick figures reaching out for

future image changed by virtue
of lit floss as if a studio
had dubbed the figures
action sticks in dunes
as caves and have nots
evenly occurred in time to tune

falling silent across stone
d walls above troubled water un
bridged figurines stopped not
ation action beyond such past
oral gestures to some wish
ed for rig of truth drilled in

figurative rigs bring
trouble that arrives stillborn
in gestures true to
walled posthumous
dabbling in young wishes
adjusting to the stoppage

screened troops in
formation and the errors
coded bright on green
or is it what remains
some torn leaves branches
whacked (as an) aside

from founding paths
for foundlings to escape
raw pilgrimages apart from
signals that shade pulse
from raw to mainstream
turns toward sense and stone

d is ability to read the tied
turned arm awaiting fool
s gold turned to lead again
or sewage as a river
to step across / the trip
trap down in drugs all avail

able telegraphy rug deep
seeping with river
turned raw beneath the steps
trapped fated imprints
signalling to lead
toward traps

toward taps
as signalling loss
leaders read faith
fully inscripted encrypted on
warped signs slaked in
sewage dumped from the top

to trick
le down as
nature s s/hill in
tended all things drizzled over
the unwary masses led
by facts of slight

sleight of hand
some is as does nothing
knows nothing comes from
nothing citizened on that hill
above what lonely crowd imagine
hanging not hinged on fear

specular research gone walkabout
deserts of mind fielded
beside a slow light wave
particled existing breath of
each day lost again in in
dustrial noise silencing

wing beside mimed breath
becomes the pale field
of inbred ex
pectation crosses infield
repeating the conviction
stamina is always silence

a quietude expecting nothing not
ing spaces breath might make
against a clear sky air burning
colder as cooling might flares
thoughtless convictions bent
awry in that explosive Truth

unsettled letters im/pose

fractions of the worth

in see through cold

where canticles emerge

against always against

sky s own Pacific

xlvii

chalk / chaff / loosened from
surface concrete / diminishes
concrete as though whittled to
staccato bits equivalent in lore
to what is
rumoured to be real

carried on the winds
snaffling those words dusted
across floors deadened to all
sounds / lost articulations of
what must be forgotten in every
(un) sanction / the echoes waver

(in)articulation chafes the sensory
infraction in which sanctity s a silver
tone amid threshing sonorities
that fill the rooms and yards
whole towns previously
mute now offer a shrill wording

as if smoke on the horizon
were orisons offered to a sun
gone down in dusty acknowledgement
dirt poor rises from machines
harvesting only quietude
lost cry for succour (sucker)

succulents hold still
against horizon as though
offering their poverty
equal to or greater than
the normal harvest
immune to the machine

mechanique deceptions slash
each kernel of ruth expanding
into the rind of ring of
losses windblown
across roads no more
barren or driven hence

alignment a lie of the machine
a wish to steal third face
facing roads driven from
windblown sand paths
long turned quiet
lines across

redcrossings as if inscribed
knowledge could bleed in
to one page after another
floated on a blasted heat
turned to darkened silent
ill iterated beyond that loss

age crosses each iteration
of darkness that repeats
the diminution of turned page
adjusting silence to
a loss inscribed
on psyches

turning their own pages
on as if lit from behind
behind tentative inscript
inscape scraped away
for what lies
beneath or above such speech

luck spatters against sprawl
of equator s circuitry remanded
to mere turning thought
lofty from the distance
that protects each being from
chance scrapings beneath

low slung engines glower too far
across bridges hanging too loose
sparks flashing neatly oiled
packing such trailing obfusc
into suburbs of scabbard thought
clouds hide what would be wielded

trance of rain trails cloud
to bridge sparks engineering
a mere ruse close to
packing hidden blades
that fit neatly into
oiled places far from yield

115

going nowhere but how slowly
cut into swathed field
seeded potential gone down
to ash swept aside in backwash
spilling something too anti
personnel found wanting there

the seeds accumulate
and fields include them
stage on stage sunshine once
swept where moisture thrives
backwash eventually diminishes
potential of person number gender case . . .

thrashing to the timbre of plane
geo frostless call to cull from
falling and then fallen rows
once green precision behind
intention blue reprise blue sentenced
blue to white as growing wall

rising always up to
what exact shade of
blued steel wall through
which each white line
marks but a trace of
fire fall disappearing

with a flitter of the line
the line s own place
would outer each pulse
opposite of stalling to
ward hypothesized
infringing upon

nought (as if pro
nounced above
ancient fields too
green and pleasant
gone to future dust)
mirrored bent below

wave precis
limber and
the old and tend
er lengthened width
of space pleases
in green a future

capitulated whimsy s racing
heartsure future   such
source error s lights
the nexus of polling aqua
in tent s berating colour
fronds all in between

twinned tours of dark
nested in caverns ousted
on laddered canyon walls
flashed with such east
exploded light   night
blooming   petalled inside

lit crepuscular thin
mauve link in chain of
daily dalliant thought
how caved in the motive
power falls to dust
bones crumbling buried there

into the fields forcible
masking daylights beneath
which caverns draw in
cast die thrown
the hidden stones after
each loss traced down

feeling possible airs
contingent breathing
cavernous cool/warm breezes
slight shivers tending to
ward any waft out
come the dark denies

an early morning
that refocused breeze
apart from shivering
to find refreshment
after dream
and whole inside a day

xlviii

half moon/lighting the nonce
naked thought trans
lated littered across dimensions
that hidden buds of this formerly
remembrance lying drowned
and growing under ground

spondee s ground break
weighs what buds that cross
dimensioned thought would
weigh remembering
a highlit moon pressed
into service

staggered turns of
phase fast moving feet
fall into metric shade in
flayed trees throwing
silhouettes dancing lightly
on piles mulching mallecho

chief among mishaps
light staggers between
matrices   sown motion
into stasis clunked in
piles of phrase amounting
to a measured mulch

a fallen trunk diseased into
an attitude inscribed
where heavy words will
eternal empire / power
never fallen into disuse
rust as active exchange denied

all use acts changed
with ease as attitude s internal
flower s trusted to imbibe
an atmosphere that s prior
to imagined heavens
true as nerves and tendons

cramp stretch grapple
muscling into stasis star
fall through rabbithole infinitude
almost black light careening
inward ghostly gravitas
holding areas aglow

muscles recall the past
in plural and endure
the pain postponed from previous
harmonic touch and now
only these threads
of contact linger

hovering as ghostlight
shines strands around
the musculature of pain
held off held onto heart
reach deep reach unto
bloodrun still beating song

lenten reeling vetoes drumbeat

or allows   sad caverns

hold those passed   if present tense is real

which present tense does one

adopt   the silent one

the irretrievable

the turn toward requiem slow

beat judders an inner drum

head down   breathtorn

bloodfrenetic tension

caught in a lie   life

lost silence knots speech up

being meanwhile in the body

equals sensing caught breath

of the other holding on

to breath yet shallowed

loss is inner turn and largo

as the rhythm s blood goes dark

tuning circadian beats to

the light dark turn of

douce massage / how

the air above vibrates

and each slow swell

builds through the lungs

she holds in check   expulsion

of breath to voice   so little

there she saves   awaiting

an allowance   the time being

sacrosanct   that scarce

arrival   soon away

and each inhalation   her beat

ing heart held back   what each

we sees   each individual

breathing eye   of the heart

felt accommodation   awe

fully left   exiling exhalation

beholding   being held

we separate   for survival

presumed a gift

we embrace   logistics

who will arrive   when

dis simple things   like this

embark   distraught taught

a kind of holding   on

to every hard won breath

lessening   levering

concern up   that such care

given   returns   unlost

morning   then an after

noon   the play of

voices   recognizable as

care turns   difficult

because of   only patterns

help   one step   toward another

one breath at a time   taken

into a silent   falling off

flicker   daze   nights

weave close   waves of

ways of   remaining near

retaining tears   held in

each particle   a re
traction   of days qua life
time   single cell   close to
prismatic   making its own
retrospective   weaves
in silence

in silence
breath tells takes
in the air accountable
as affective   days
nights   flutter of
shadows   shaken

amid gray mist
diminuendo   sure voice
dreamed back to equal
light of eyes   that still draws in
small histories even as hope
begins to shift away

as frail as broken
pieces   dry and quiet
beyond context   loss
of hope or leaving   thus allows
a stalled endurance to be
hymn   for all the recollection

held against time s recon
ciliation   how days
turn   through nights above
the closing eyes of
remembrance   all those blossoming
stars   how they open out

colour of wind colour of

charred place   sesqui scented

aftermath   equivalent to

simplicity   closed eyes

spinning   before   reducing time   ·

to something chiselled thus   made small

xlix

few   silences
match weave   of high thought
beat   braced
muscular   night pelts
substance   of rigour tuning
forth from each   brass bell

pulled and   tossed notes
bray   break   against
rock   echoing
water muscled   twist
of wave   particles
silence thrown out   inhere

wait   list to
one side or real
it ties   wist
full longings   long
evities   how
hear that lightfalling through

pace itself   these mar bled
flecks of   shine lines
strong   in pat terns
swollen in   magnetic
form as   forms
long for   these t ides

antlered   /   crashed
crushed into other
hoped fors   how
a run at branches
leafstrum   flickerblur
bluer   shades drawn in

as if to quell the strum
of damage kept qua
tonal repartee   each branch
mutes   the ambient noise
while adding brush chase
to these window panes

pan demonium shakes
rattles white watered
glass hall pre empted
steam streaming off in
clouds of demonstratus / thunder
argues   flashes quod vide

roll saffron s aftermark
less pastiche   reams of
cloud   *dimanche* under
the threnody   emptissimo
new sea spackled
with halls in lashes

sound translation enforced
administration   bureau or auto
cratic decisions reminder of
remainder remonstrates wreck
age   old ways held to
send youth to keep dying

uninterrupted   seashine
silver blue   as if
cross stitch   ordered
a way   to mark
the loyalty   as long as
anchors hold

against what rising seas
off   shore or sure
yawl   caught up in
tsunami insistence what
mis apprehension   no
appreciation of other loss

no sure seas catch
dark wind   leaning
long into   the rise again
scapular wing approaches
over and across a yawl
that moves toward insistent shore

taken in too far beyond
beyond far / length of tossed
home / ward or bound
gone / how the natural
uns into legal straits
stretched beyond hope

that the tided wish
wash sways some
tiny motive movement / eyes
eying something beyond
mere individual human
pain swamped

where purity once
was   swaddled around
bodies   beyond
imagining   this
inhuman   truth
that begs   amnesia

forget full blues greyed
in the tsunami washout
as if memories of
of   of   notes
tossed upon the waters
letters ran to nothing there

letters   waters   blank
place on earth
amnesia tru
ncates   habit
worn on full   in full
infill   as if

too much the real in
trudes   truth tracked
by fact found gone
under   riding a slow
tide   silence in the head
a void (losing game / face

off e ring a new line
back to factual lowdown
a quaff of dunder may
haps   screened or
torqued or ridden
true to feat (to form

a new the way out at
last at lant is
pay meant new venue
ventures / from retreat
and loss to loss and
treats re price conversion

treat dross as silt
normed outer layers
craft rice into prima
facie fie
lds   consume acquire
reside you all where best

goes fast to worst &
fie sir leads to no stir
ring of fire or water
earthing down   as into
pan (dem) ic   the ice
of compassion commuted

I

suspension   b/locks keep
sakes leading to   belief
in elements   like ringing
lyre brushed hand
some   ping un
leashing pandemonium

free jazzing wind
instruments against what
savaging wave
as faithbase fails
fate bashes heartbuilt
paved desire   sung or sunk

sprung tines spling when
precipice of for ever holds
just for the nonce be
fore the lashing savage f
ails to be queath
the needed instrument

science feels when it is science
whole   when it is true
faith is irrelevant   good science
falls together   rule based
trumps a rhythmic inter
face off   with the deep dark thickest walls

reasons not the need here
say what deduced   evinced
in evi and prece
dence   those slight trails
frozen now in muddy
stone   waves of deep time

at an angle even   outliers
might align   the given
telling past whatever form
of water   paper water
said the bureaucrat   just a list
of possibilities   as continuance

one speaks in prime numb
ers(twhile) holding still
to find words   seeking
stretch beyond
the old illogic
of unlikely story

bodes mo(mentum) yet to
come unbidden mayhaps
mountains having stood with
stand unlabeled stacks
of surfaces driven awry
and well beyond a knowing

131

a geological smirk or stacking
odds and endings   lay
ered eradications   fall
en angles off peak in
dications of godsspeak
ing mudslides   spill of

stone work tending
contraindicative rides up
filling space   red
comma blond comma
white before the change
in nature turned to mimic angles

as if as if stutter reflects what ah
wide wingspans whip of eye
stormed rush of in or un
witting writing on the skin
of earth ripped awkward
awry   tree alphabets torn

wingspan s sterling
chisel of earth skin   mars
surface and tips   inhabitants
as alphabets qua tottering
inflections sore from
tall momentum

monumentum falling
as implosions re
treat inward heartsoul lost
faith foundered   un
tucked   falsified
calcified   broke right down

improvised moment by
minute shifts of opinion
s siren songfest   fist
full dollared loss less
summed against than
swimming in it   necessarily

one hypothesizes a move
meant to piece song from
sums provisional although
imposing losses
shifted from
fest to fist and pining

(st)rips the tide fantasia
through veins no longer gold
though blooded on a crescent
(s)word not savage but
suspect   lies lay a body
bare   beyond sculpting hand

gratitude warm as gold
a crescent of propriety   sure
act of art   changes the body
(chastens) in a blood wide street
through long elapsed
fear points as though some sacrifice

always necessary be thanked
even as corrosive fire falls
from a sky so lately blue
notes wafting on heatwaves
their scorched scorching words
unread by the charred remaining few

simultaneities chafe pure souls
(poor souls) dreamt by takers
as fair game   lately
no amount of rinse suffices to remove
the waft of crime   depleting
even thin hypotheses of something clean

what left behind might wash a soul
away that voted for a fact
oid voided blind belief
held holdings banked for
futures unbeheld / hype
theses thinned by thought less

ashen foal left in field
a distant systole prior
to abandonment   an act
of severing soon thin
life force existing
not at all perhaps for reasons

of states of impatience states
of lying states sans being
told and untold s
cars that burn by fueling
half life right stained
states injurious as slung

boyish bravado
s not enough as
the accident slithers
in flames across more
freeways undone in
untruth s telling evidence

plain and here although not
lithe   neither accidental nor
free the way the telling might
of this bravado s
inks its way in
to the psyche s very s ore

afterword

Emmylou Harris, talking about her collaboration with
Mark Knopfler, made a point that allusively applies to
our work on *Continuations*: 'When you combine two
unique voices it creates a third, phantom voice.' Over
the years, as we have continued writing this odd serial
poem together, it s that continuing discovery of the
third voice that has excited us.

Collaboration tends to encompass a wider reach than
individual work typically does, although no such rule
is constant. We have liked each other as collaborators
because each of us has managed to balance his/her
own uniqueness in service of the shared creation.

One of the delights of this collaboration has been
our broader sense of subject; there is less sense
of tightly controlled 'about-ness' to the process.
Concepts, referents, even possible sites of imagery,
are alive, balancing the roles of receiver and sender in
a two-way process where the 'music' of what s being
produced provides much of the charge. When writing
collaboratively, there s a comfort and a simultaneous
'ready for anything' sensation, as the spectrum of
surprise and expectation is touched in various places.
On seeing or hearing the other s response, each of us
is often stimulated by the passage just received and
read, then drawn into the work by wanting to respond.

This leads to the blurring of lines between writers alluded to above. Thus, the better the collaboration, the less evident the two (or more) writing styles. Rather than a lowest-common-denominator approach to writing, ideally, collaboration brings into being a new writer, different in many ways from either of the individual writers. Such a presence cannot be forced into existence. It comes with committed working together over time.

In *Continuations*, we agreed on a more or less fixed format of six lines, and have bounced the ongoing process of poem-construction back and forth over the years, since November 2000. It seems that in that time a 'third individual' (Emmylou Harris s 'third, phantom voice') has emerged, who writes differently from the way either of us would independently.

Some 'joinings' are so natural, so easily integrated into one s working style, that they become part of oneself. Working on *Continuations* feels to us so vital and interesting as to have become so much a part of one s day that there has been no impulse to stop.

The sense of this has much to do with some of the approaches that we both would call language writing: the ways in which it invites its practitioners to collaborate with pre-texts, to play with and through the many inheritances carried in the words one uses. Collaboration invites precisely this kind of writing with and back to the other(s) involved in the process. So it seems that, in such writing, one can give up (or give up to) a more open sense of subjectivity, one in which something more like the 'Martian dictation' Jack Spicer talked about occurs between the collaborators. Ideally, the work should appear to belong to an other than any one of those involved.

What this says about 'individuality' or 'the subject' is complex and beyond the purview of a short statement on our work together. Nevertheless, it seems pertinent to mention that not only have 'we' 'chosen' (although we have never discussed this nor made what might be called a 'conscious' decision on the matter) not to introduce an 'I' into the poem, but we suspect it would be very difficult for a reader to manufacture one that would fit the conventional lyric speaker of a poem. We have used an 'I' in some sections, but it s really just a 'figure' ('of speech'), a grammatical action, only. What we have done, we think, is refuse/refute the conventional singular 'I' of lyric poetry, even as we have sought to hold on to a lyric melopoeia, the rhythm of, the music of. But *Continuations* eschews the normal 'personal' perspective, hoping the language leads the reader to perceptions not given so much as enacted, displayed.

Time passing, the period over which these poems were written, back and forth as e-mail, enters into them as a context that infiltrated the writing process even as we (consciously) thought to evade 'the world,' and its way, through attention to language as such. But in fact, one of the layers of language implies, in various and varying ways, political and cultural passages of the period during which we wrote this together.

The return on collaborative endeavours has variously taken the form of (1) a unique feeling about making

137

something, of (2) a stronger, clearer point of com-
monality with a fellow writer, perhaps a deepening
friendship, (3) a joyful sense of accidental accomplish-
ment that exceeded one s expectations, (4) a seamless
work that one can hardly recognize having been a part
of, or some combination of those four. On returning
to read sections of collaborative work, it is particularly
satisfying not to be able to discern which of the part-
ners wrote which section or line. When that happens,
it may well mean that things were clicking.

Sheila E. Murphy and Douglas Barbour

acknowledgements

Thanks to Peter Midgley for jumping at the chance to
see this second volume of *Continuations*, for finding
two such sensitive readers, and for seeing it through
publication, and to Cathie Crooks and all the staff at
University of Alberta Press, with whom, once again,
it has been such a pleasure to work.

Thanks also to Kevin Zak for his elegant design.

The authors wish to express thanks to the editors
of the following publications, where some of these
poems first appeared: *Jacket, The Drunken Boat,*
poetics.ca, *Shadowtrain, Fiera Lingue.*

139

Other Titles from The University of Alberta Press

Continuations
Douglas Barbour & Sheila E. Murphy

116 pages | Essay on collaboration
A volume in cuRRents, a Canadian literature series
978–0–88864–463–3 | $19.95 (T) paper
Literature/Poetry

Poets Talk
Conversations with Robert Kroetsch,
Daphne Marlatt, Erin Mouré, Dionne Brand,
Marie Annharte Baker, Jeff Derksen, and
Fred Wah Pauline Butling & Susan Rudy

216 pages | Notes, bibliography, index
A volume in cuRRents, a Canadian literature series
978–0–88864–431–2 | $34.95 (S) paper
Literary Criticism

wild horses
rob mclennan

96 pages
A volume in cuRRents, a Canadian literature series
978–0–88864–535–7 | $19.95 (T) paper
Poetry/Canadian Literature